snapshot·picture·library

ENDANGERED ANIMALS

snapshot · picture · library

ENDANGERED ANIMALS

FOG CITY PRESS

Published by Fog City Press,
a division of Weldon Owen Inc.
415 Jackson Street
San Francisco, CA 94111
www.weldonowen.com

WELDON OWEN GROUP
Chief Executive Officer John Owen
Chief Financial Officer Simon Fraser

WELDON OWEN INC.
President, Chief Executive Officer Terry Newell
Vice President, International Sales Stuart Laurence
Vice President, Sales and New Business Development Amy Kaneko
Vice President, Sales—Asia and Latin America Dawn Low
Vice President, Publisher Roger Shaw
Vice President, Creative Director Gaye Allen
Managing Editor, Fog City Press Karen Perez
Assistant Editor Sonia Vallabh
Art Director Kelly Booth
Designer Andreas Schueller
Design Assistant Justin Hallman
Production Director Chris Hemesath
Production Manager Michelle Duggan
Sales Manager Emily Bartle
Color Manager Teri Bell

Text Thomas Downs
Picture Research Brandi Valenza

A WELDON OWEN PRODUCTION
© 2007 Weldon Owen Inc.

Library of Congress Control Number: 2007936045

ISBN-13: 978-1-74089-653-5
ISBN-10: 1-74089-653-X

10 9 8 7 6 5 4 3 2

Color separations by Sang Choy International, Singapore.
Printed by Tien Wah Press in Singapore.

Today, many unique animals are in danger of dying out. These creatures are known as endangered animals.

Luckily, through the efforts of people all around the world, some animals that were once endangered are growing in number again.

Learning about these amazing creatures can help us to take better care of them and enjoy them for a long time to come.

Gorillas are
very smart.
Some can even
talk to humans,
using a simple
sign language.

Other primates are also very smart. Langurs, howler monkeys, and orangutans teach their young how to make tools.

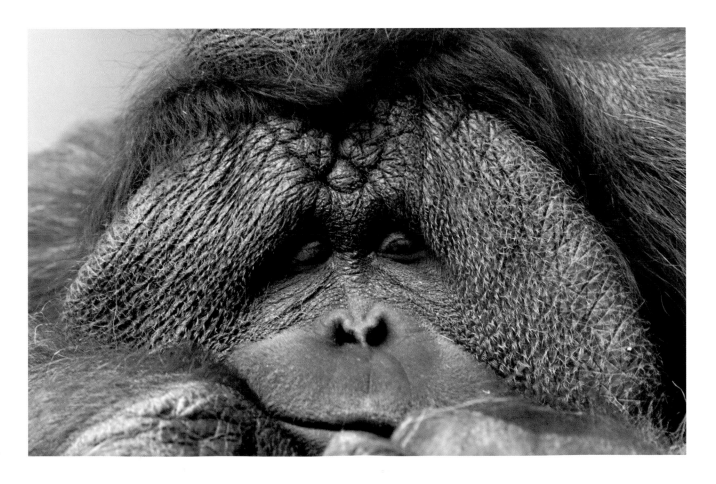

If you look into these animal's eyes, they always appear to be thinking.

Most of the time, they think
about how to get food, and how
to take care of their young.

Lemurs and langurs are at home high up in trees. But for the red panda trees are food.

Some animals like to stay near the tops of trees. They need to be in large, thick forests, where they can move from branch to branch.

Clouded leopards feel right at home on big tree branches. They can even climb upside down, underneath a branch, if they want to be sneaky!

Other cats look for food on the ground, in wide open spaces. They are able to run very fast.

Burrowing owls, green turtles, and cheetahs all have spots—all the better to blend in!

These owls have different colored spots to help them hide in different places. Can you tell where they live?

Birds of prey live up high. From there they have a bird's eye view of the small animals they hunt and eat.

The ibis and the hornbill have
long beaks to catch their food—
under water or even in long grass.

The toucan has a very colorful beak. Toucans live in wet and humid rain forests.

Most frogs live
in wet areas
too—some in
rain forests,
some in swamps
and rivers.

Reptiles can be found from the ocean to the desert. These reptiles like to spend time in wet places, like mud pools and rivers.

Dugongs live in the sea but they stay close to land. The scars on this dugong may have come from a boat.

Water pollution and lack of food can also cause problems for ocean animals, like humpbacks, orcas, and Hawaiian monk seals.

Even animals that live in the water as well as on the land, are affected by changes in the ocean and water ways.

Bengal tigers with black and white fur have always been rare. Today, there are fewer than ever. Many people are working hard to try and change that!

So many animals are black and white, even though they live in very different parts of the world.

These bears have different ways
of hunting—from the ground
and under water.

It is difficult to catch a glimpse of a brush-tailed rock wallaby, a bactrian camel, or a tiny tarsier. All of these animals are very rare!

Even though
horses are easy
to find, truly wild
horses are only
found in Mongolia.

Ibexes, gazelles, and antelopes have been hunted for their beautiful horns. Now, they are protected in national parks.

Other horned beasts can survive
only if their grasslands are not
used for farming.

Not everyone agrees on which endangered animals are cute and some are not even that friendly...

...but would you really want to say good bye to the last pygmy hippopotamus?

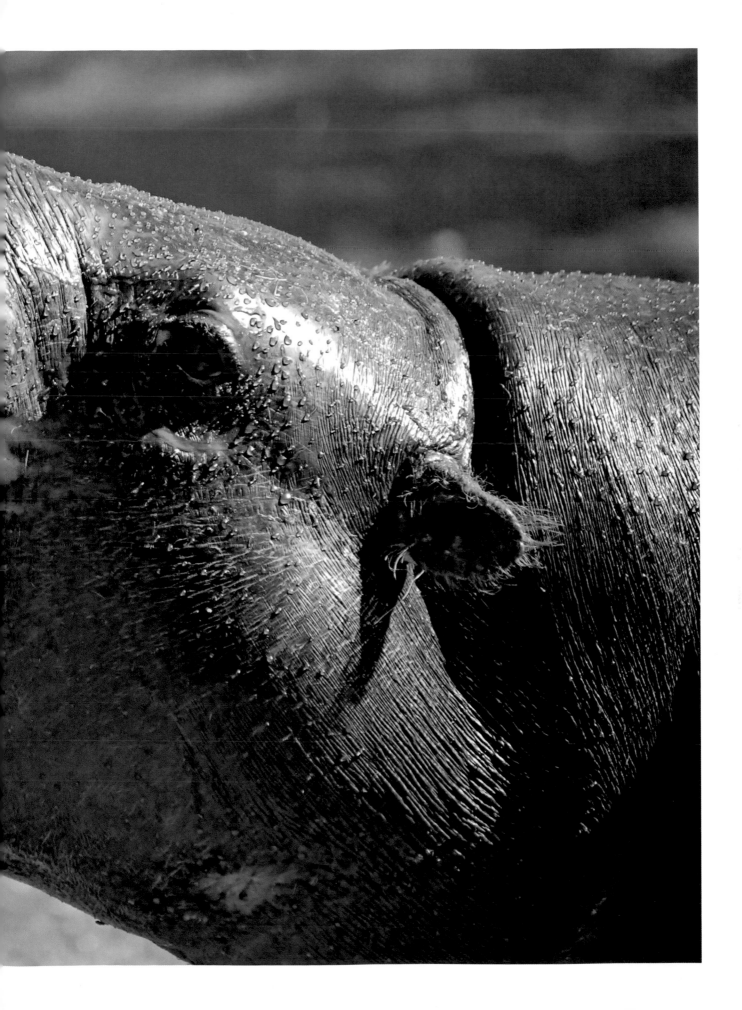

Orangutan
Borneo, Sumatra

White-Faced
Saki Monkey
Parts of South America

Burrowing Owl
Parts of North
and South America

Silver-Studded
Blue Butterfly
Parts of Europe

Red Panda
Nepal, southern China

Green Turtle
Parts of Atlantic
and Pacific Oceans

Sea Otter
North Pacific

Black Lemur
Madagascar

Cheetah
Parts of Africa

Mountain Gorilla
Democratic Republic
of the Congo,
Rwanda, Uganda

Ebony Langur
Parts of Indonesia

Snowy Owl
North of the
Arctic Circle

Hanuman Langur
Parts of Asia

Crowned Lemur
Madagascar

Eurasian Eagle Owl
Parts of Europe
and Asia

Black Howler
Monkey
Parts of Central
and South America

Pygmy Three-
Toed Sloth
Tropical Central
and South America

Great Gray Owl
Parts of northern
North America,
Europe, and Asia

Orangutan
Borneo, Sumatra

Koala
Australia

Peregrine Falcon
Worldwide,
except deserts and
polar regions

Hanuman Langur
Parts of Asia

Clouded Leopard
Southern China,
southeast Asia

Harris Hawk
Parts of the Americas

Sacred Baboon
Parts of Africa and Asia

Lynx
Scandanavia,
North America,
the Himalayas

Ferruginous Hawk
Western United States

Mandrill
Parts of Africa

Caracal
Africa, western Asia

Scarlet Ibis
South America,
Trinidad, Tobago

Long-Tailed
Macaque
Parts of Asia

Snow Leopard
Central and
southern Asia

Southern Ground
Hornbill
Parts of Africa

Toco Toucan
Parts of South America

 European Edible Frog
Europe

 Marsupial Frog
Parts of Central and South America

 Red-eyed Tree Frog
Southern Mexico, Central America, and northern Columbia

 Galapagos Giant Tortoise
Galapagos Islands

 Gila Monster
Southwestern United States, northern Mexico

 Tuatara
New Zealand

 Dugong
The Indo-Pacific, northern waters of Australia

 Humpback Whale
Oceans worldwide

 Orca
Oceans worldwide

 Hawaiian Monk Seal
Hawaiian waters

 Humboldt Penguin
Chile and Peru

 Hooded Merganser
Parts of North America

 Gentoo Penguin
Sub-Antarctic islands

 Bengal Tiger
India, southeast Asia

 Giant Panda
China

 Black Lemur
Madagascar

 Grevy's Zebra
Eastern and southern Africa

 Polar Bear
The Arctic

 Kodiak Bear
North America

 Brush-Tailed Rock Wallaby
Australia

 Bactrian Camel
Eastern Asia

 Tarsier
Southeast Asian islands

 Przewalski's Horse
Mongolia

 Ibex
Europe, Asia, Africa

 Grant's Gazelle
East Africa

 Bontebok Antelope
South Africa, Lesotho

 African Buffalo
Parts of Africa

 Gemsbok Antelope
Parts of Africa

 Black Rhino
Eastern and Central Africa

 Warthog
Parts of Africa

 White Rhino
Parts of Affrica

 Pygmy Hippopotamus
Western Africa

Asian Elephant India, Sri Lanka, Indonesiaia, Sri Lanka, Indonesia

ACKNOWLEDGMENTS

Weldon Owen would like to thank the following people for their assistance in the production of this book: Diana Heom, Ashley Martinez, Danielle Parker, Lucie Parker, Phil Paulick, and Erin Zaunbrecher.